# RUN
## with your
## dreams

Written by Maureen A. Burns
Illustrated by Dorothy Rackliffe
Foreword by Og Mandino

In memory of Ruth Bommer who told us,
"Go home. Get your dreams off the
shelf and do something about them!"

Dedicated to Danny, Colleen, Donna and Cara.
May you always run with your dreams.

# FOREWORD

*Run with your Dreams* is a marvelous book. I loved it! Using a bright format and illustrations, it is one of the finest and most powerful tools to change your life for the better that I have read in many years. It's a dream-reviver of the first order.

God bless,

Og Mandino, *author*
*The Greatest Salesman In The World*

# PREFACE

We live in a fast paced world with stress, indifference and much negative thinking. This book is written on a positive note meant to uplift and inspire people. It is a book to be enjoyed, shared - good to read but better if used and applied. We have chosen child-like art to illustrate because we feel strongly that the child in you is your most creative part and should be kept alive and vital. This book is aimed at changing lives, inspiring people to dream creatively, mold their dreams into realistic goal plans and progressively work until they achieve them. This process may seem new and difficult but please try. The most serious failures we make are when we fail to try, not when we try and fail. If we all would reach a little higher in our lives we could form a more positive world, one with less stress and indifference.

Please read and use this book as it is written - with joy, optimism, seriousness and dreams. It is not meant to push people into the direction of the "me generation/philosophy" but rather to promote personal growth of individuals within the scope of their own lives, while gently caring, loving and respecting those around them.

*Maureen A. Burns*

Maureen A. Burns

*Dorothy E. Rackliffe*

Dorothy Rackliffe

# It all begins with this!

*"But I can't see anything!
It's empty."*

*"You can't see anything because . . .*

*. . . it is full of room. Room for you to grow. It is you. Your gift of life, your potential, your talents dreams, goals, pain, joy, your person."*

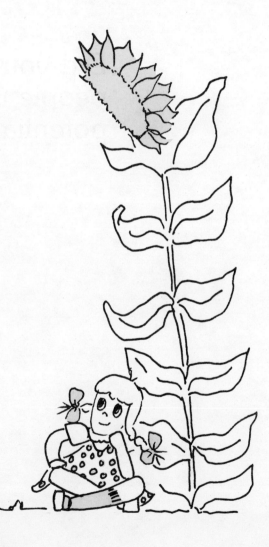

Did you know that most
people use only 10% of their
potential and 90% goes
d
o
w
n
the
d
r
a
i
n
.

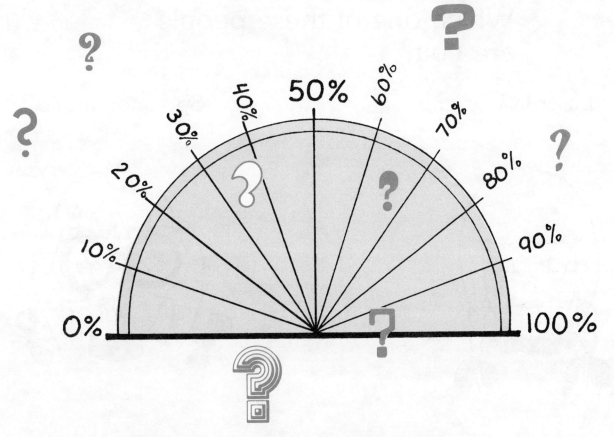

On the scale of life, how
much of your potential are
you using?

# Which one of these people are you?

Loser in Life

Spectator in Life

Wondering
what happened.

Watching things
happen.

Or are you a
Winner in Life / a Do-er

Making things happen!

Everyone loves being a
winner, enthused, excited, and exciting.

Winners dream dreams,
set goals,
work to achieve their goals,
dream more dreams
and
run with them.

# FACT of LIFE

You gotta have a dream
if you're gonna make a
dream come true!

Give yourself a dream.
Get excited!
Get enthused!

Put action into your dreams.
Make them realities or you
might just dream your life
away.

You have the

POWER

to make dreams
come true,

HOWEVER

you will have to work at it.

Do you live in the past?

I could have . . .
I should have . . .
I wish I had . . .
I might have . . .

Have these negative words
locked you in?

Do you live in the future?

Someday I'll . . .
I have to . . .
I ought to . . .
They're negative words that can also lock you in. They sound safe but reality never comes.

**NOW**

is the only part of life you can control.

This moment.

To be a winner profit from the past, live in the present and look to the future; living a continuous positive cycle.

Remember

*You are who you are TODAY !*

When you look in the mirror
do you like who you see?
Do you like who you are?
  The friend you are?
  The parent you are?
  The mate you are?
  The child you are?
Do you want to live with this
person 24 hours a day for the
rest of your life?

Have you tried all you want
to try in your life? Have you
seen all you want to see?
Study your normal route.
Perhaps now is the time to
explore an unfamiliar road.
Try a new avenue, a
challenge.

# LIDS

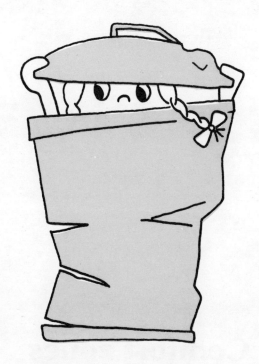

People put lids on
themselves.
    For example -
    Saying no
    Avoiding risks
    Being afraid
    Staying in their
        comfort zone.

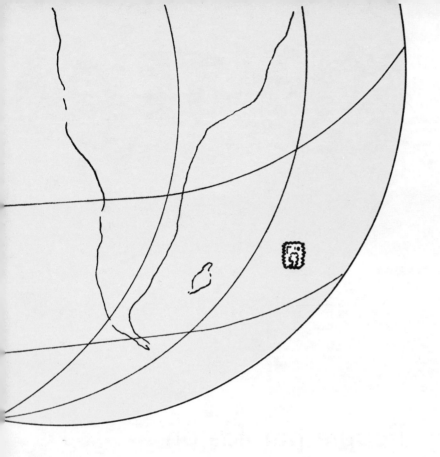

## **Comfort zones**

can be as big as
the world or as small as a
postage stamp.

**Saying**

- stales you, closes you to life.

Try yes - it refreshes you and opens you to life.

# RISK

Reach higher than you have before. Remove that lid!

Touch a cloud with your dreams.

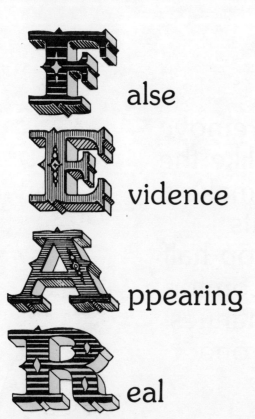

**F**alse

**E**vidence

**A**ppearing

**R**eal

Do you say, *"I never have . . . What if I can't . . . I don't know if . . ."*?

Have the courage to remove your lid. You can be like the caterpillar who dares make a major effort to reach its potential. It doesn't stop half way when it has the comfort of the cocoon but continues pushing forward until one day it emerges into

a beautiful

*Let's get personal.*

Dag Hammarskjöld said,

"THE LONGEST JOURNEY
IS THE JOURNEY
INWARDS!!"

Try filling out the following exercises. Be honest with yourself and give each one serious thought.

Words I wish described me-

_____

_____

_____

_____

_____

_____

_____

_____

Compliments that
mean a lot to me -

_____

_____

_____

_____

_____

# Some positive aspects of me

| My appearance | My personality | My character |
|---|---|---|
| _____ | _____ | _____ |
| _____ | _____ | _____ |
| _____ | _____ | _____ |
| _____ | _____ | _____ |
| _____ | _____ | _____ |
| _____ | _____ | _____ |
| _____ | _____ | _____ |

Of everything in my life,
I am most proud of

_____

_____

_____

_____

_____

_____

_____

_____

_____

_____

_____

_____

_____

_____

_____

_____

_____

_____

_____

# Things that I value in my life -

# What keeps me from achieving my dreams

_____

_____

_____

_____

_____

_____

_____

_____

Circle every one you can do something about.

Is your life planned? It should be. To work toward fulfilling dreams you will need to set goals.

How you set your goals
depends partly on where you
are when you start.

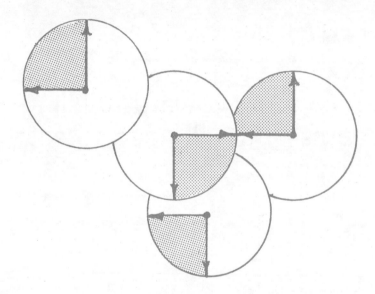

Are you in the first ¼ of your
life? Half time? The last ¼?

Setting goals is like bathing.
It is unending. You cannot
take one bath and think,
*"There, I am done with that!"*

Both baths and goal setting
are for
the rest of your life.

Rules on goal setting:

Goals should be *realistic,*
*flexible,*
*updated often,*
*prioritized*
*and*
*have a deadline date.*

# Are you ready to list some of your goals?

Lifetime _____
_____

5 Year _____
_____
_____

1 Year _____
_____
_____
_____

Immediate _____
_____
_____
_____
_____

Share the thoughts of an 82 year old looking back.
One wonders what goals had been set.

*If I had my life to live over, I'd try to make more mistakes next time, I would relax, I would limber up, I would be crazier than I've been on this trip. I know very few things I'd take seriously anymore. I'd certainly be less hygienic. I would take more chances, I would take more trips, I would scale more mountains, I would swim more rivers, and I would watch more sunsets, I would eat more ice cream and fewer beans. I would have more actual troubles and fewer imaginary ones, you see, I was one of those people who lived prophylactically and sensibly and sanely, hour after hour and day after day. Oh,*

*I've had my moments and if I had it to do
all over again, I'd have many more of them.
In fact, I'd try not to have anything else,
just moments, one after another, instead of
living so many years ahead of my day, I've
been one of those people who never went
anywhere without a thermometer, a hot water
bottle, a gargle, a raincoat, and a
parachute. If I had it to do all over
again, I'd travel lighter, much lighter
than I have. I would start barefoot
earlier in the spring, and I'd stay that
way later in the fall. And I would ride
more merry-go-rounds, and catch more gold
rings, and greet more people, and pick more
flowers, and dance more often. If I had it
to do all over again --
but you see, I don't.*

Anonymous

Death is democratic. It doesn't care who you are, what you're involved in. It strikes unexpectedly whether you are ready or not. This moment - NOW - is the most precious thing you will ever own. All the world's wealth cannot buy it. It is a pure gift. It is yours.

Heaven can NOT wait. When
you arrive do you think they'll
ask

*"Why didn't you cure the
common cold?
Why didn't you end war?"*

More likely they'll ask you . . .

. . . "With all your potential,
With your huge gift of life,

**WHY DIDN'T YOU
BECOME MORE OF YOU??"**

Who is responsible for your
life, your dreams, your goals, your action?

Is your mate ?

Your family ?

Your friends ?

Your community ?

41

# NO!

*Life is a do-it-to-yourself project!*
You are responsible for the success or failure of your own life. You can't blame others. Even God allows you the freedom to make your own choices.

You must hold on tight and *run with your dreams.*

Even if sometimes you fall,
get up and keep going.

Failure is a part of life. It shows that you are doing. Doing is growing. Growth is winning. Use those failures as stepping stones to your goals. Your dreams will be achieved
one moment at a time,
one step at a time,
one hour at a time,
one day at a time.

## Look To This Day

Look to this day, for it is life,
the very life of life.
In it's brief course all
the realities and verities of
existence, the bliss of growth,
the splendor of action, the glory
of power -
For yesterday is but a dream
And tomorrow is only a vision.
But today, well lived, makes
yesterday a dream of happiness.
And every tomorrow a vision of hope.
Look well, therefore, to this day.

Sanskrit Proverb

Act as if you were already
living your dream. Act as if
your goal was a reality. Your
state of mind is crucial
because your mental attitude
determines your success.
You talk yourself up. You
talk yourself into everything.
Your imagination is the key to
your world.

No one ever said life would be easy. It isn't always - but it is still possible to achieve your dreams with commitment.

Spend 30 minutes each day
on your dreams, on yourself.
Find a quiet place (perhaps
your pillow at night) and
mentally picture as vividly as
you can your dreams and
your goals. See them as real.
See them clearly. See them in
detail.

*"I can.*

*I want to.*

*I am.*

*I will.'*

Experts say it takes 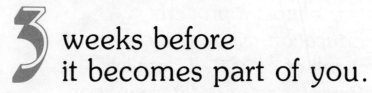 weeks
for a person to adjust
to something new,

weeks before
it becomes part of you.

# PRESS ON

*Nothing in the world can take the
place of persistence.*

*Talent will not, nothing is more
common than unsuccessful men
with talent.*

*Genius will not; unrewarded genius
is almost a proverb.*

*Education will not, the world is
full of educated derelicts.*

*Persistence and determination
alone are omnipotent.*

Anonymous

Remember - you are in
charge.
You plan your own trip.
You scale your own
mountain.

It is up to you.
Don't end your life with your
dreams buried inside of you.

Turn your dreams into goals,
    then add action.

The dreams you put off will
   never happen.
You do them now or you
      may do them never.

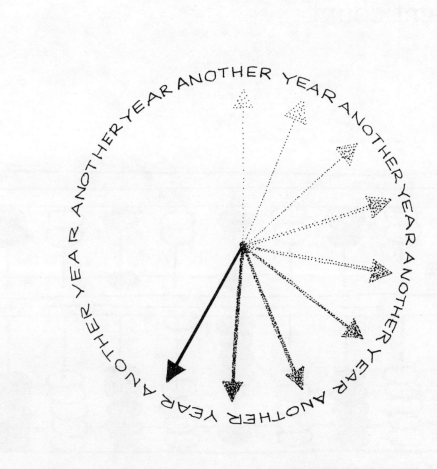

The clock of your life is ticking.

Make each moment count
for you.

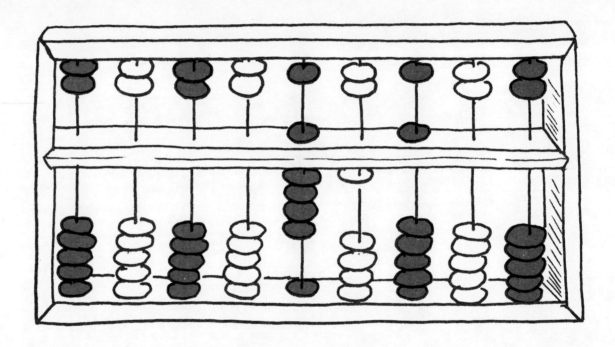

Enthusiasm keeps you going.
Get enthusiastic about you.

Keeping the promises you make to yourself is as important as keeping the promises you make to others.

# NOW

spend some time
thinking over what your life
means to you

and then . . .

Run with your dreams!